W9-BIC-781

Light Waves

Light Waves

☙ ☙

Fine Tuning the Mind

☙

David K. Reynolds

A Latitude 20 Book
University of Hawai'i Press
Honolulu

© 2001 University of Hawai'i Press
All rights reserved
Printed in the United States of America
06 05 04 03 02 01   5 4 3 2 1

Library of Congress Cataloging-in-Publication Data

Reynolds, David K.
Light waves : fine tuning the mind / David K. Reynolds
p. cm.
ISBN 0–8248–2378–8 (pbk. : alk. paper)
1. Spiritual life—Meditations. I. Title

BL624.2 R48 2001
291.4'32—dc21
00–057690

University of Hawai'i Press books are printed on acid-free
paper and meet the guidelines for permanence and
durability of the Council on Library Resources.

Printed by Versa Press, Inc.

One wave moves and ten thousand waves follow.
—Keizan Jōkin

Trying to subdue a wave by striking it
only results in a thousand waves.
—Morita Masatake

Contents

Preface

The reflections below were stimulated, in part, by my reading in a particular form of Zen Buddhist religious literature. But the reflections themselves are neither religious nor Buddhist, as I see them. My apologies to Keizan Jōkin (1268–1325) or whichever Sōtō Zen writer actually put forth the *Denkōroku* (A Record of the Transmission of Light), which has been translated by Thomas Cleary as *Transmission of Light (Denkōroku): Zen in the Art of Enlightenment* (San Francisco: North Point Press, 1990), and by Francis Cook as *The Record of Transmitting the Light: Zen Master Keizan's Denkōroku* (Los Angeles: Center Publications, 1991).

One characteristic of the following style of writing is its sudden grounding of poetic flights in the actions of everyday life. No one lives within a continuous stream of peak experiences. Everyday life is both ordinary and marvelous. While sailing your mind in the sky, don't forget to have your car serviced regularly.

Acknowledgments

I wish to thank the Okamoto Memorial Foundation for its annual support of my work in Japan. I am also grateful to the families whose current and historical existence allows my work. Finally, to those who taught me words, and to whatever puts words in my mind, I am grateful. My debt to certified Constructive Living instructors in Japan, North America, and elsewhere cannot be expressed in words.

1

ক্ষ ক্ষ ক্ষ

Appearances

*B*eauty is in the eye of the beholder. So are love and hate and flowers and garbage and the beholder herself. So is the eye. There is only the eye, and it is all eyes.

Winning and losing, too, only have meaning in terms of spectators. What is the sense of winning if no one is looking, not even yourself? Better just to keep your fingernails clipped. I used to win nearly all the contests I entered until it became clear that there are no contests. All the while my fingernails kept growing. Now clipping, clipping. Out of sight is out of mind. Out of mind is out there somewhere anyway, keeping the fingernails growing. Or so it would appear.

A student once asked me, "What is the purpose of having a purpose?" Another student asked me, "Can one be mindful of being mindful?" I answered them both with my eyes. There are only eyes, after all. Only one word is sufficient, and the eyes have it.

Number-crunching and word-crunching are essentially the same pursuit. The codes are built in; they come with the system. The answers are already worked out by the time the rules are formulated. Whatever grammatical calculations you try, the results are foreordained. Language requires you to come up with certain mental totals. Can it lead you to a new way of counting? If not, you must go beyond the alphabet to spell out real numbers. Thinking in itself won't get you there. Floors must be swept and meals prepared. Greetings and thank yous and apologies and farewells are part of the process of seeing the eyes with new eyes. Purposeful effort is essential in recalculating life. Count on it.

2

ॐ ॐ ॐ

Whose Mind?

*H*ow do I know that you know what I know? Yet
sometimes we smile in recognition of that fact.
In that moment it can be said that we share one mind.
Whose mind is it? It is the mind that perceives fingers
and clenches fists and dances to mind music. However
carefully we scientifically trace neural patterns, we
never find that mind, though it is that mind itself which
is tracing the neural patterns. It is that mind by which
you read these words. It even makes sense to say that
these words are that mind. But then, so are the words
on a cereal box when you read them (and when you
don't).

Reality never leaves you; ask any scientist. God
never leaves you; ask any Hindu or Jew or Christian.
Old Śākyamuni Buddha is with you always, say the
Buddhists. Everywhere you go, there you are again.

You can't make purchases using someone else's

credit card. You can't fly on a swallow's back. You must mow your own lawn. Studying with a famous teacher or attending an eminent university or entering an élite corporation or writing a best-selling book doesn't bend Reality's rules. The fresh moments keep coming.

These words aren't my words or your words or words from some figure of the past. They are whipped cream in a downpour. Watch them decompose and flow away. Do your life well in the downpour. Put out the trash and wash the car. Those who do so are performing miracles. Miracles are feats no one can successfully explain. Miracles are everything you do.

I don't pass anything along. My job is simply to stir up the waters where they may have settled too long. That task keeps our feet wet. I, too, am amazed at what gets churned up. Better put, one kind of churning is amazement. Now settling, settling.

3

⅌ ⅌ ⅌

What Is Mine?

*W*e all walk nested in tradition. The mother taking care of her child represents her own mother and her mother's mother. The lover moaning in ecstasy joins human and other animals throughout history who cried out with pleasure. The Zen student who bows before entering the zendō follows a recognized tradition. To use the word "satori" or "enlightenment" or "Zen" is already to be flooded with old whiskey that cannot be mopped up or dried off. Beware the smell of whiskey or King James or psycho-pop or Constructive Living on your breath.

Pointing to the watering can may acknowledge the can's existence, but it doesn't get the plants watered. And we can't water one another's greenery. It is vital that you find some way to water your own plants rather than standing around admiring the verdant fields about you. About you. Standing around admiring.

Think about it. And remember that your own plants are no more yours than the water is yours. So whose fields were you admiring?

We are all composed of space, linked miraculously to the bodies we find closest at hand, the ones we call our own. But the "me" drifts around in a clouded sphere of attention wondering where it really belongs, while knowing that it cannot find a home in any place. Location is as meaningless as time to this "me," though it can make up stories about both (as when it feels "my" heartbeat).

What do you call yours? Fail to pay your property taxes and discover who owns your home. Your body becomes ill and refuses to obey your commands. Life savings pass on when you do, perhaps before. Families grow and scatter. Possessions and minds wear out. Life rusts.

4

࿇ ࿇ ࿇

Fixing the Mind

*W*e only borrow. We are all always in debt. Offer thanks for this moment. It holds what we cannot hold, but can become.

Magical powers are like millions in the bank. They pull attention into trivial ventures. Trying to maintain a salesworthy face or public attention is equally short-sighted. Beware small successes that inflate ego and dreams. You really can't get there from here. And if you do, by chance, arrive there, then you can't get back here or there again. The trick is to pay attention to where you are now.

Analyzing your psyche is an expensive parlor game, costing more than money. As time passes most people wake up to some degree and get on with their lives, whatever games they play. Blanking your mind is static overlaid on a potentially clear frequency. Educating your mind can be a martini or a magnifying glass, an art film or a road atlas. Despite all your imaginings, what you know is right before/behind your eyes. Something answers when you are called. Something puts words in your mouth. Something walks your legs and determines where to go. Something makes sense of these words. The meanings are "given" to you. Created and creating, the psyche plays in the ocean on fissured sand.

Some try to fix their minds with their minds. They try to mold water to hold water. They blow against the breeze. It's better to change what you do, and give the mind a chance to respond. Get feedback on your actions from Reality. Sweeping your kitchen affects the dust on your soul. Your mind doesn't belong to you any more than your kitchen does. We are all "in transit." To expect a fixed destination is to miss the boat.

How do you expect to find your mind with words while those words compose your mind? Defining words by words keeps you in the word world. When I tell you that *this* is Reality and Reality is all there is, then I am only wording you. Experience the Reality that the word points to and the word disappears, or rather it slips back into its word-reality. Surely, whatever I tell you is wrong. I'm genuinely sorry about that inevitability.

If you seek peace of mind or a life free of anxiety or self-confidence or endless joy or boundless love, you toddle after pretty words. Doubting happens, sorrow occurs, delight arises, anger emerges. They aren't annexed to your psyche; they are you, that momentary you. There is nowhere for you to hide from grief or pleasure or concern. They don't chase you. They are you, that momentary you.

So when you see this matter, who gets credit for seeing it? It is no more than this matter seeing itself. Or did you see it at all? If you are looking back on the experience, it is hard to tell. More words emanating. However you want to describe it, salt tastes like salt.

5

৯৯   ৯৯   ৯৯

Reality Teaches

Reality is your teacher. If you seek enlightened human teachers or spiritual masters, they are no more your teachers than your toaster or a chipmunk is. Even their talk is likely to be no easier to understand than that of the toaster or the chipmunk, though it may sound better to your ears. Reality teaches you personally with endless lessons using a myriad of teaching aids, including other humans. You have earned these lessons by merely attending class. They are your birthright. They can be ignored, but not with impunity. There are consequences to being a good student or a bad student at any moment. You can't cheat on Reality's exams. Reality is never fooled. Pay attention! Your mind's intimate teacher teaches itself.

Being ordinary is both easy and extraordinarily difficult. Those who are ordinary see themselves as nothing special. How could they be special? After all, there is only this moment and what it brings that needs to be done. Noticing what emerges and acting on it are everyday undertakings, unworthy of special consideration. Yet within this process wonders abound. Where? Who? How? Why? When? have no real meaning here. The questions don't apply. The available answers are only disguised questions that arise from the ground and fall back to it. How we love to rearrange words!

It's never too late to discover the present. The older we get, the better chance we have to learn to wait. As babies, we wanted our needs satisfied now. As we age, we learn that nows hold much more than merely satisfying our hunger. Letting others go first also needs to be done, sometimes. No matter what age we become, Reality keeps generating new information for us.

6

꙲ ꙲ ꙲

Reality-Presents

*I*t's amazing that Reality comes to me, is brought to me. The me it comes to is also brought to me, or at least brought. Why do you suppose there have been teachers through the ages who pointed to Reality? If they didn't appear for you, then for whom do you think they existed? Do you think it sufficient to simply acknowledge their teachings and ignore what needs doing? You can't know the depths of their teachings unless they permeate your body's actions.

Life has no chapters; life has no scenes. We construct the commas and periods in the sentences of our lives. Truly, there is only one long utterance. The meaning shifts from moment to moment. Inhale, exhale, inhale, exhale. Kathump, kathump, kathump, kathump. Thank you, Reality. Do you find such talk grammatically correct?

Certainty comes and goes, too. Like love. Again

and again. If you don't like the weather now, just wait a few minutes. This weather report comes to you courtesy of Reality. Weather is all about you.

Why do you want to know these things? What causes you to read and ask questions? What prompts you to turn over these matters in your mind? What is it that accepts or rejects the conclusions you reach? You can say that something thinks you or that thinking happens or that thoughts appear from nowhere. Why, then, do you call them "your" thoughts? Because thoughts about "you" appear, too? Images of you as a child, memories of your young adulthood, visions of you in the future all contribute to the possessiveness exhibited toward your thoughts. The images, memories, and visions are gifts, too.

There are many ways to explain why things are as they are. But however you wish to believe things came about, don't abandon Reality for fantasy or oughts or hopes or ideals. Always start from where you really are, wherever you want to go. However you wriggle and squirm, there is no fooling yourself. In this Reality we are the same, we are rather alike, we are different. We are all the means by which Reality realizes itself. We humans all share human characteristics. We all represent particular social, local, familial, and personal cultures. All you ever have to work with is the way things are.

7

ॐ ॐ ॐ

Doing Reality

*Y*ou need not wait to learn these lessons perfectly in order to teach them to others. Your life has been a series of imperfect accomplishments. Unshared and untested wisdom wastes away into emaciated word forms. So offer your borrowed learning to Reality's representatives and learn again from the response. You don't need to be a sage to see what's so clearly before your eyes. Sometimes "sageing," sometimes not. Sometimes seeing, sometimes not.

No one ever lived alone. No one ever lived self-sufficiently. Not even the mountain monks. You can't pay your debts by running away or by frightening others away or by hiding yourself away. You must pass along what you have learned. So you must first learn something worth passing along. Then you must find someone who will learn from you. In relieving one debt you incur another. Of course.

What can I say about Reality that isn't also word-reality? There isn't any way to get outside it to point at it. I just stir it up and watch how the patterns change. What stirs me to stir it up? Consider that question, please. Then ponder your pondering. Now stirring, stirring. Round and round.

8

꤮ ꤮ ꤮

Reality's Fools

*B*orrowers become thieves when debts go unpaid. Borrowers of respect are no less thieves when their debts go unpaid. You came into this world naked and dependent on others for your very life. Little has changed, has it? Wrapping your body in stock certificates won't ward off death's chill. Endings, like beginnings, are out of your control. Once warned, twice *sly* won't pay off in the end because there are so many endings. Investigate the balance of your accounts while they are still open. No one ever committed fraud and got away with it. Come clean now.

Something gives birth over and over to itself. Something re-introduces itself to itself again and again. Recognition is the goal. So be aware of Reality. Notice the shifting reincarnations of seasons, of days, of moments.

Often I don't understand the reasons. Often I have neither time nor capacity to explain. Nevertheless, there is no denying what is. What is keeps following me around like my body warmth. It envelopes and includes me. It remains flawlessly real whether I like it or not, whether it fits my ideals or not, whether it makes sense to me or not, whether it hurts or pleasures. I must acknowledge it whether it is convenient to do so or not. "What is" is neither outside me nor inside me; it pervades what I call "inside" and "outside." I cannot stand outside it and call it anything. Anyway, I'll call it "Reality" or "God" or, not so simply, "what is."

9

⚜ ⚜ ⚜

No Boundaries

𝒜 box has an inside and an outside. No matter how big you conceive it to be, there is an outside to it. So there can be no box big enough to house this whole Reality. You know that, but do you *know* it? Boxes are forms made up by forms for forming. Fortunately, no one can box you in. No psychological test, no psychiatric diagnosis, no praise or curse can box you in. Such boxes are no more than forms made up by forms for forming. They are real forms, real boxes, but they cannot contain you. You always overflow outside them. Raise your lids and look inside and out.

Boxes have histories. We refashion our personal-history boxes again and again. It is important to recognize the tools and purposes with which we reshape our personal-history boxes. The histories they contain and the histories of the boxes themselves are both worthy of examination. You have always spilled over beyond the bounds of every one of your personal-history boxes. You have always exceeded your tools and purposes. You have always gone beyond yourself. Nevertheless, plugged toilets back up and dead leaves fall down and burned-out light bulbs don't illuminate. What's for dinner tonight?

10

ॐ ॐ ॐ

Making Sense of It

What good would it do you to know what you used to be? In some past age, some babyhood days, last week, a second ago? You are not you-then; you are you-now. What you-now does is infinitely more important than a gift-wrapped box of personal history. To be sure, Reality contains you-then as well as you-now. It fits the interlocking puzzle pieces into the whole of you because it contains all the pieces to the puzzle all the time. You can search for yourself by introspection, but you will find only a sort of slice of yourself there. There are many more slices to be sliced. Move your eyes and ears and fingers and other body parts to slice them. No matter how it is carved, the whole remains complete and tasty.

What occurs is merely the playing out of what happens. We color happenings with evaluations and judgments and misjudgments (or so they are judged).

You can't really conquer yourself. You can't really win or lose at life. We make up rules or borrow them and play our own games to provide ourselves with winning and losing hands. Consider your games carefully; choose relatively harmless rules and tactics; offer prizes to others; play fairly. All the while know that you are being played by Reality. Or, if you prefer, you are playing out Reality. Our minds are built to make sense of happenings, no matter how senseless the understandings. Our minds are constructed to discern justice and injustice, good and bad, right and wrong, powerful and powerless, no matter how senseless the discriminations. It may be useful to explore others' discriminations and understandings with an eye to modifying your own. At any rate, please do your best. Losing yourself in doing your best is a very fine way to avoid entangling yourself in pondering these matters of evaluation.

11

꙳ ꙳ ꙳

Ideas in Action

*T*aking pride in humility is fatuous. Punishing your body to attain some spiritual goal is a hobbling hobby. Heat blisters; scratches bleed. No mysterious merit accrues to the hungry and exhausted and tormented. Use what Reality provides, for Reality is using you (to reconstruct itself over and over again). Of course, wasting resources is wasting yourself, diminishing yourself. Simply be realistic, be factual. You already have riches beyond counting. Come to appreciate the state of your welfare. To work for the best is admirable, but it is the working and not the best that is meritorious in itself. Fit yourself into Reality's jigsaw puzzle; dissolve yourself in Reality's chemistry; float on Reality's breeze. While humility and anguish and aspiration gust about, hold to your objectives and move your body.

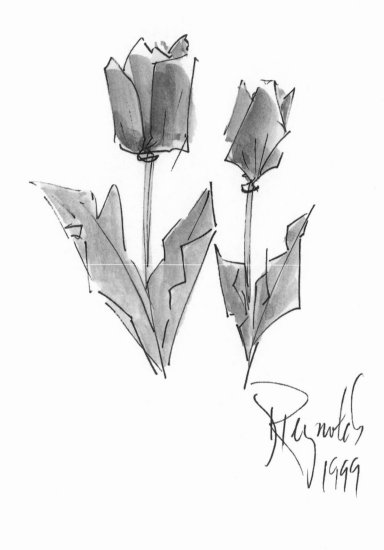

Rich or poor, the chances of applying these principles are equal. Male or female, young or old, no special consideration is forthcoming. Something within you asks about life's meaning. Something within you solicits your best. Something within you interprets failure. Something yearns for merging. Something makes sense of all this variation. Something keeps shifting. Something steers you toward the light. Something. You.

What is left over when people go away? Ideas of people. Memories, dreams, judgments about them. We write letters to ideas. We reminisce over photos of ideas. We visit the graves of ideas. Have you discovered yet that we need not be apart to do so? Ideas are all there ever was. Make no mistake: ideas are real ideas. There are no happy memories, but we are really happy when remembering some events. Ideas happen. Events occur. So we exist.

Where is your mind? What does it look like? When did it begin? How does it end? Such questions emerge from ideas about ideas. At least I *think* so. You see colors painted on your mind with eyes painted on your mind (via light waves painted on your mind). You become colors. Do you *see*? Anyway, be sure to keep your room-idea clean and rake the idea-leaves of autumn. Become constructive action.

12

క్రం క్రం క్రం

Practicalities

*W*ho can escape Reality? Neither by mysterious alchemic incantations, nor by spiritual proficiency, nor by chemical flotation of the mind can one escape Reality. You are presented with this world of television and cellular phones and mosquitoes and drunk drivers and cancer and stocks and football. If your mind freeze-frames one aspect of this ever-changing variety, you chill yourself. Don't become obsessed with the eyes of others, with pulsations, with accumulations, with perfection, with emptiness. You need not attempt to stamp yourself on Reality. Just be flowing ink. Allow Reality to write itself with you. You really have no choice in that matter. However, the scope of the composition is up to you. Do well what Reality allows you to do. Give yourself the gift of actuality.

There is no fixing your mind. You would need an improved mind to begin the task of improving your mind; that condition, in turn, would require an improved mind. There is no end to that beginning. It is quite acceptable to work with what you have. It is possible to improve on what you do, leaving your mind as it is, wherever it might be. Your successes to date were accomplished with imperfection. Yes and no. To be sure, we can always find perfection in imperfection. And, of course, what I call "my" hands are moved by millions of hands.

Ancient and distant hands move me as well. Perhaps those same hands will indirectly move you, too, through these words. Writing always involves Reality's ink. Instrumentally. Don't run after magical words or trendy dudes. What needs doing now? Do it.

13

꣢ ꣢ ꣢

Dawning Light

*H*ow do you pass yourself along to others? You give away your genes or your ideas or the fruits of your body's labor. You do kindness or cruelty or indifference and thus make your mark on other representatives of Reality. Consider carefully the ways you make your mark on others, for there is no way to avoid marking. You cannot step outside the whole of it. To where would you step?

Have you ever been dead? Not that you know about. What were you before you were born? It's hard to say. What will it be like to die? You can't call on previous experience to answer. Worrying about the unknown and unknowable is a pastime for humans with time on their hands. What you know is now. Do the now well. Each moment you are reborn along with the rest of Reality. Each moment you die along with the rest of Reality. Always just this. Old or young, male or female, we are all only now-people.

You may find it useful to send messages to that person you will call yourself in the future. Of course, it is not you who will call yourself thus; it is that future person who will call yourself you. That future person will have groomed memories of what it was like to have been you now, but the memories won't be you-now. You will be gone. Already that you who read these words is gone. Forever. Please use the new you well.

The boundaries of dawn are difficult to define. Where does dawn start and end? The boundaries of you are likewise difficult to define. In time and space you merge into otherness. Your works are you; your childhood was you; your food is you, in time. Membership in Reality came before you were born and continues after you die. You leave footprints; you are footprints now.

Why do I write these words? Neither for myself nor for you. It is merely that the words need to be written. Reality always takes care of its business. Jobs get done. Whatever pride we may feel when a task is accomplished is pride on loan from whatever got the task done. Nevertheless, there is Reality's work that only you can do. Thank you from the rest of us.

14

※ ※ ※

Passing On

*H*umans may attach rankings and salaries to occu-
pations and tasks. However, there is no honest
occupation or task that is nobler or more valuable or
more spiritual than any other. Garbage collection and
diplomatic service and sewing and university teaching
and selling goods are all equally part of Reality's scheme
now. All fit within the jigsaw puzzle of what is. All
contain the opportunity for accurate, thoughtful dili-
gence. Examine your intent and attend (i.e., show up).
What else is there to do?

Babies will be born after you die. Your house will
fall apart with age. Governmental offices will be filled
by people you never met. People you never heard of
will be media stars, the toast of the town. What do you
owe the occupants of that future-minus-you? Looking
back, what have you received from past explorers and
inventors and factory workers and farmers and your

ancestors? All past and future generations of people and things are with you now. They guide your hands and your thoughts. They live you, even when you think you are all alone in the world. You are a nexus that forms and dissolves itself in an instant. This instant.

You can pretend to ignore past and future, but they comprise you. So you must use this now well. Something chooses your choices. Something informs your information. Something moves your movements. It isn't that all is preordained; rather, that all is ordaining, thanks to the whole of you. For all our sweat and struggle and sacrifice, we are lived by Reality. So please pass along life.

15

❦ ❦ ❦

Being Lively

*I*t is a quiet end-of-the-year morning in this place now. Many morning events haven't formed yet. The New Year will bring new moments. They, too, are now formless. How will Reality mold them? While waiting for events to appear, I form them. Now writing, now preparing breakfast, now going to the post office. I conduct those actions using the computer, pans, and car invented and fabricated and sold to me by others. I bought those tools with money given to me by others for work I did that was taught to me by others. The boundaries blur. While forming events, I am in-formed. The scene isn't really limited by the spotlight of my eyes. Only I am thus limited.

Knowing we shall die spurs us to use life meaningfully. Thanks to others, who *all* die for us, we are reminded of our own inevitable end. Death-knowledge colors our evaluations of money, power, status, fame, accomplishment, love, respect, and all valued aspects of our existence. However we pretend to ignore death, flee from it, conceal its inevitability, we collide with it each time we feel pain or fright.

We do more than back away from death, however. We push toward life. Something prompts us to do well, to succeed, to develop, to achieve our goals, to support others, even to sacrifice ourselves for others. Something wants us to live life so well that it nags and scolds and ridicules and endlessly prompts us toward the perfection of which we are capable. Why do what needs doing? Because something requires, even demands, our attention and effortful action. It wants the best for us. And our best is more than the delay or avoidance of death.

16

ॐ ॐ ॐ

Stop-and-Go Living

*W*e are sometimes good, sometimes evil; sometimes serving others, sometimes self-serving; sometimes thinking of the convenience of others, sometimes thinking of our own convenience; sometimes this, sometimes that. We comfort others and protect ourselves.

The changes lie in time. Timing is crucial. Try instant waiting. Firewood never becomes ashes. Green fruits never ripen. Watch for the ripened moments, the ripened actions, the ripened thoughts. You can't change a tornado's course by blowing at it or by ignoring it. You can't speed a river along by slapping at ripples or shouting at it. Get to know your rivers.

After you realize that your mind has psychological defenses, after you see how your mind safeguards your self-interest, after you know your mental tendencies inside and out, what do you do about that insight?

Discerning won't get the application filled out or improve your actions toward others. The next step is stepping. Again, seeing that next step isn't stepping. Only stepping is stepping. There is no armchair traveling.

Though the world is vast, there is only the road on which you walk. You make your road a possible course for others. So please walk carefully along your chosen path. You cannot stay in one place over time. Stopping permits reflection, but going permits stopping. In your search for a stopping place, don't neglect going. There is no backtracking.

Every path ends.

17

঳ ঳ ঳

Artistic Living

Speaking with a deep voice is not so difficult. Wearing robes comes merely from obtaining them and putting them on. Attracting followers is easy for those who play voice music. It is possible to add clumps of mud to one's hair indefinitely. Going beyond such frivolity is going beneath it. Wriggle and squirm until you can fit yourself into the dot of the I. Meanwhile, recycle old cans and newspapers; answer the telephone.

Important objectives merit discomfort and perseverance. Being ignored permits hidden development. Rebuffs and criticism permit strong resolve. Tragedy permits heroism. Restrictions permit exploration. Doubts permit faith. Wind is defined by calm. We share our shadows.

Wherever you turn for advice, only you can determine what you need to do. Whatever you admire, only you can attend to your life. Whatever our aspirations, we all fail sometimes. However we fail, a fresh moment appears. Stringing moments into life-strands is an artistic pursuit. You are an art object. Whose art object?

18

🦋 🦋 🦋

Curing Yourself

G ive me your life and I'll straighten it out? Bring me your troubles and I'll dissolve them? Show me your pain and I'll relieve it? Tell me your suffering and I'll capture it? Hand over your shyness? Submit your self-doubts? Deliver your soul? Don't be foolish! No one cures neurosis. No one imparts peace. No one heals anxiety. No one can rescue your mind. Salvation just keeps coming anyway. Discover the salvation right before your eyes.

Our world is full of people we don't know. We make guesses about them by looking at their appearances. Strangers might support us or kill us. Customers might rob us or make us rich. Languages and customs puzzle us. Politics and economics are in flux. Sickness comes and goes. Where can we find certainty? Reality is certain. Step back and step into it. Don't try to play games with Reality. It is immeasurably smarter than you are. Fortunately, you are both on the same team; you are the same team.

We can rob ourselves. But Reality always apprehends us. Why put out effort to steal from yourself? Thieves don't understand what belongs to whom. We forget what doesn't belong to us. Despair, timidity, and pessimism are caused by forgetfulness. Anxiety and panic are fundamental lapses of memory.

"All right, Reality, I'm ready." That's the proper attitude. Keep your mind-weight balanced. Lean neither forward nor back. Watch for what comes up next and deal with it realistically. Nothing holds you back. Recognize hunger as hunger, attacks as attacks, possibilities as possibilities, facts as facts. Act practically based on this gift of discernment. Avoid tying yourself in knots, tripping yourself, meandering. There is just enough information for your action in this moment. Perhaps your necessary action is to seek more information. Informed consent, informed dissent—who decides? Who molds that flood of stimuli into meaningful flavors? Taste Reality.

Scour the tub, close the door, phone your mother, dry your socks, comb your hair, mail the letter, buy the groceries, wash your windows, fold your pajamas —just do it. Taste each act as spiritual, as mundane, as self-growth, as drudgery, as voluntary, as prescribed. Anyway—just do it. We all add spice to our lives. Your main course is doing. In*deed*.

19

๛ ๛ ๛

Reality's Pool

C an you swim against the current without getting wet? Not really. But getting wet is not so unpleasant. Just splash. And drip. It is actually possible to shift the course of the current ever so slightly by your effortful swimming. That shift is possible because you are not separate from the current; you have never been dry. No one ever stood on the riverbank and watched the current flow by.

I can't teach you how to swim. My swimming style is imperfect; how could I coach anyone else? Nevertheless, you know how to swim already. So avoid being obsessed with learning how to swim. Just swim toward your destination. While doubting, while agonizing, while worrying, even while giving up, just keep swimming. You'll surprise yourself at the distance you've covered.

Books about swimming technique dissolve in

water. They may impede your strokes. Such a warning won't stop you from reading them, however. Floating while reading is a hobby, even a profession, for some swimmers. Again, please keep swimming. Now I seem to be swimming while treading water.

We get stuck in familiarity and comfort. Even obsessions and fears become old buddies. We hesitate to risk what we already possess in order to achieve something beyond the usual. Yet we possess nothing at all. To set out on a new course is an individual matter. To offer to accompany another who undertakes this new course is a worthy task. Go along and then turn back so your companion can proceed alone. Over time, even well-suited wheels rust and impede progress.

Receiving praise is no great accomplishment. Quietly go about your business of life. Let praise pass through like rainy days. Collect the rain and pass it along to your teachers and students and colleagues. Sunshine or rain, know that you are doing Reality's deeds, accomplishing Reality's tasks. Just pound nails and sift flour.

For there will come a time when you can't.

20

や や や

Shopping Around

*P*erhaps you think there are steps or plateaus or stages in developing your constructive life. Such an analysis is constructed by your mind and has Reality only as a mental construct. You are just this now—sometimes absolutely perfectly in accord with your ideal, sometimes not. Missing this point is like writing a feature story about ancient Bethlehem's crowded inns at Christmas.

You may be told that enlightened people of old were deeper, more disciplined, wiser and more upright than you. Don't watch retouched videotapes of old television commercials about products no longer for sale. Buy Reality today.

I can't know your suffering. I can't even remember my own past suffering accurately. Words drive us along the highway, but not in the same cars and not to the same places.

21

ॐ ॐ ॐ

Storytelling

*T*he mind is a storyteller. It tells stories about neural shots in the brain at night. It tells stories about events and stories about stories. It tells stories about individual words and stories about combinations of words. But the mind is not the neural shots and it is not the words and it is not the stories. This story is about the mind-story.

Suffering people make up stories about their suffering. They create origin-stories from their childhood and stress-stories from their current lives. The stories these days are primarily borrowed and adapted from popular storytellers who live in the lands of academia and medicine and the media. Stories may provide a temporary sense of understanding and control over a life that includes suffering. But all stories, including scientific stories, are varieties of fiction. They are creations. It is possible to shift from one line of stories to another quite readily. What do you think of this story?

While slipping and sliding around the ice, just skate toward your goals. Believe it or not, goals keep popping up. You can't stop them from appearing, even if you try. Goals, too, are presented to you—you've heard that before. Stories offer information about where to look for some goals, so be careful about the stories you adopt. The draftier the story, the draftier the goal, and the more difficult it is to know if you've reached it because you find yourself being blown about. Skate close to the clear ice. Discover your affinity to ice. We are all ice-skaters.

22

ॐ ॐ ॐ

Reinventing Yourself

*W*hat causes you to want success, to desire to contribute, to seek to grow? What causes you to
feel fear, anxiety, loneliness, boredom? What causes
your interest in these topics? I tell you it is neither your
brain-sparks nor written words that cause this interest.

To make your mark in the world you must find
solid ground, a base for your work. To fail to do so
merely produces spinning wheels and fruitless effort.
Find your traction. You can go back to it when fatigued
and disillusioned. You can tread with it when depressed
and empty. The base provides a guideline for knowing
when doing is not doing and when not doing is doing.
Remember that meditation is merely another form of
doing and not doing.

Seeing yourself as though outside yourself is different from seeing this page. Responding naturally to
the ringing of a phone is different from making your-

self answer the phone. Making yourself make yourself answer the phone is different yet. Watching yourself make yourself make yourself answer the phone is stepping farther back. The more complicated it gets, the more likelihood of paralysis. You can immobilize yourself with thinking. Don't you think so? You program yourself with meta-programs that program themselves with meta-programs that program themselves endlessly.

Impulsive, unconsidered behavior may be hurtful, too. Good habits, measured routines, and familiar circumstances may keep you on track. They may also promote boredom. Nibbling at the edge of your groove may be the solution. At any rate, grooves keep writhing. Notice the twists and turns. Discover who notices.

23

ॐ ॐ ॐ

Reviewing Yourself

*W*hat do you know already? Why did you come here? Where do you want to go next? You can read these words from a thousand miles away. Or you can pour them over you until they seep into your soul. Talking about improving your environment on the one hand and actually weeding your garden on the other are quite different endeavors. Watching a video of Japan and visiting that country are far from identical activities. Identify what really is.

The milk carton and ballpoint pen teach us about balance and impermanence and design and function. The telephone teaches us about time and information. The double windows teach us about stillness and clarity. Nonverbal teaching is available to the silent student. Keep eyes and ears open. Your faculties are surrounded by faculty. Make the connection. Re-educate yourself.

Interpretation, evaluation, judgment, and memory —they all lay a grid on Reality. The grid may be useful or not. Beware when the grid lines become so dense that the underlying Reality is obscured. Don't let self-conscious evaluation of your own successes or failures interfere with your noticing your circumstances. Observation protects you from excessive wording which takes you far away from your own feet. I can't help you find yourself. You were never lost, though you may have thought you were. Right here you are, surrounded, all alone.

24

☙ ☙ ☙

Meaningful Construction

$\mathcal{N}$ aked Reality doesn't care about oughts and should-have-beens, but you do. Fair and unfair, right and wrong, success and failure, hopes and regrets make no sense to a Siamese cat. Such distinctions, however, will enter your mind. Welcome them while sorting the laundry and counting your change. To try to defeat them is to be drawn into shadow-boxing with yourself. Become acquainted with fears and disappointments and apprehensions, however disagreeable they might be. Let them accompany you on your travels toward your various destinations. Because they are going along for the ride, they can't produce detour signs to sabotage your trip. Keep driving on. Your companions will certainly help point out the scenery to you. And the bumps in the road will transmit their messages as you drive. For all your worries about making the proper turns, something keeps your vehicle in motion.

Something causes you to keep learning, even when learning is not your intent. Your inner and outer surroundings keep teaching you whether you are prepared to learn or not. How kind of Reality to make our world a classroom! Sometimes we even recognize when we are being tested. Study yourself by looking about you. You are never too old to learn life's lessons because lessons always take place now.

Something collects and filters information. Have you noticed that? Something turns pulses of energy into a glow of meaning. No one knows how that shimmering transformation takes place . . . just as it is taking place now.

25

๛ ๛ ๛

Brand Names

*L*abels are anchors. Anchors can keep ships from drifting into shallow waters, but they can also prevent ships from sailing out of port. Anchors aren't ships. So you are not who you say you are. You are, in fact, nameless. Even the "you" is an anchor, not a ship.

Furthermore, anything at all you say about yourself exhibits equal error. Labels such as hurting, fearful, angry, honest, responsible, tough, weak, lonely, bright, stupid, and skillful are all well-known anchors. Psychiatric diagnoses are medical anchors dropped in insurance ports. Doctorates and titles and licenses are social anchors signifying only approximately where ships used to be. Weigh anchor lightly. Have a good trip.

Most people most of the time prefer anchored ships to free sailing. Beware! I just attempted to drop anchor on you. Did you notice? Or did it sail right by you?

Who, then, are you?

26

⅋ ⅋ ⅋

Situational Fusion

$\mathcal{W}$e cannot live by a formula. Any rigidly sched-
uled life sacrifices the convenience of other crea-
tures of Reality. Season life to taste with a changing
menu. Fit yourself to situations as they arise. Beware
of blindly following recipes that don't look like recipes.
Are you reading a disguised cookbook now?

Parental love applies to everyone. All humans are
your children. All cats and canyons and wood chips are
your children, too. You make them real. You taught
me all I know. I have not shifted "yous" here. The you
of which I write is really you. Thank you.

What is there to transcend? You can't get over a
lost love or even get over yourself. You have only this
circumstance, this feeling, this memory, this hope, this
goal—this Reality. Limits come with fences built into
each moment's situation. You can't get outside from
inside or inside from outside. Notice the fences and

move ahead. Fences merely mark temporary boundaries. You don't need anyone else to help you tear
down the fences. You don't need to tear them down
yourself. They are like national boundaries drawn on a
map. Run your finger across those boundaries on the
page and nothing stops your finger. Walk across a
meadow and pass from Ohio into Indiana. Where did
the boundary go?

27

※ ※ ※

Have It Be the Way It Is

*H*ow wonderful that you criticize yourself! How admirable that you care what others think of you! How wise of you to fear possible danger and anticipate potential failure! Wanting to succeed at life, to accomplish goals, to achieve survival are fundamental sources of satisfaction and misery. If you are already a person who seeks improvement and regrets ruin, then you are already a person who seeks improvement and regrets ruin. What is there to change? Satisfaction and misery come intertwined through comparison. While waiting your turn, change the light bulb and water the fruit trees.

There are steps between looking and seeing. You need more than eyes. Something mixes and matches in order for you to see anything. All you see is what has been interpreted for you. It is cooked and served to you in a flash. The brain is the oven, not the cook. There is only cooking.

So see the sights and hear the sounds and feel the feelings. Note the flavors and the finitude. Something interprets the interpretations, something knows what needs doing. Just do it. Thoughtfully, carefully, considerately—just do it.

To act rashly is to ignore some of Reality's messages. To be immobilized is to fixate on receiving only a select set of Reality's messages. To be wise is to use Reality's messages to guide action.

Please distinguish among listening, hearing, understanding, and accepting. Please distinguish among the sound of the moon, the sound of crickets, the sound of a mother's voice, and the sound of genuine laughter. Find a way to verify what you accept. Hearing words from someone else is not sufficient verification in matters of how to live well. Reality is trustworthy. Accept Reality as it is.

28

꒶ ꒶ ꒶

In Trust

*M*y virtue is borrowed. What donations I make, what services I perform, what sacrifices I offer —all are merely reflections of what has been given to me. The efforts I make to improve myself all carom off models and guidance and information and energy from my environment. Self-esteem and self-pride result from ignoring Reality's generosity, rather like foolishly taking credit for a grandparent's childhood. This borrowed life must be returned some day. How can I think of it as mine?

It is just as absurd to try to paste yourself onto some billboard of a movement or profession or religion or race. Your identity doesn't come from any of these billboards. Neither does your salvation. For all the social support and income and attention and information and privileges you receive from being a group member, you remain invariably alone in your thoughts and feelings and actions. You cannot even share these directly with anyone or anything else. The consequences of your thoughts, feelings, and actions trail after you like clouds of moments in a dusty desert. You reverberate within Reality.

Thus, while taking no personal credit and all personal responsibility, march forward as Reality's primary flag-bearer. Publicly decorated or not, you are a legend in your own time.

29

ॐ ॐ ॐ

Thoughtfulness

$\mathcal{R}$eality generates information about itself and passes on that information through eternal nows. You, too, are a kind of information. You are information regenerating itself. So discover the best way to brush your teeth. Floss both teeth and mind. And teach the children.

We are as old as we think, but not in the way most people think about it. Whatever you believe, leaky heart valves remain leaky heart valves; clogged arteries are clogged arteries. Thoughts don't age, though minds appear to do so. You need not believe the myths of persistence. Before you know it the toothpaste is gone.

Noble thoughts, heroic thoughts, charitable thoughts come and go. Put arms and legs on them. You can test their worth by acting on them. Untested spirituality is a fantasy park. Play at your own risk. Having your ticket validated by someone you respect is reassuring but not essential for entering or exiting a park. Better than riding the roller coaster is picking up trash. If you must climb the magic mountain, keep a clean park.

30

ॐ ॐ ॐ

Redoing Yourself

*W*ho is in your family? I ask not about the family into which you were born, but the family to which you belong. We adopt families by growing them. We adopt a self the same way. We become what we do. We can literally redo ourselves. Herein lies realistic promise for the whole family. Perhaps these thoughts are becoming familiar to you already.

When you know how things are, that understanding is reward in itself. You can investigate new information by juxtaposing it with Reality. You become solidly grounded. In a world of quick flicks of news and snap snippets of discoveries, you need a measure that flexes. Spring into life.

Reality appears at its own pace. You can rush yourself, but you can't propel circumstances faster than their naturally responsive gait. So use your time while waiting. Prepare, organize, reflect. Eager or not, fearful or not, prepared or not, you know that Reality keeps coming.

In these days, also, many people are just getting through time. Life isn't always easy for anyone. Standards differ. Find purposes large and small, distant and present. Find objectives personal and self-sacrificing. Find meaningful work. Mental exercises are not enough. Put your mind/body into your tasks. The tasks become you, in both senses of the word. Putting out effort in itself makes an activity worthwhile, whatever the outcome. While hoping for the best, while desiring results, don't be put off from action by failure or success.

My body moves me. Your body moves you, too. Don't forget it. It is possible to make a variety of mistakes should you think something other than your body moves you. Travel to New Mexico and see whether your mind goes along. Quiet your body to quiet your mind. Move your body to keep your mind active. Your mind is the ax that splits itself from itself. Ax and timber are one.

31

৵ ৵ ৵

Driving Yourself

*D*oubts are fine. Doubting your doubts is also fine. Doubting yourself doubting your doubts is no problem. While riding your merry-go-round, keep walking straight. While bouncing your mind, move toward the goal. While fumbling your fears, advance toward the end zone. It is neither necessary nor helpful to stop the game to deal with your mind. There is no time-out in life. Play the game with attention.

One learns to ski over time with effort. Worthy understanding may come in a flash, but long preparation precedes it. You don't tame yourself overnight or over weekly sessions with a teacher. The effort begins when getting up and ends when all goes slack. Savagery is unbecoming. If you won't be civil, go live by yourself. Do you think it possible to live all alone? Recognize and work on paying your debts. Arrogance is merely nearsighted idiocy. So is any notion that anyone is self-sufficient.

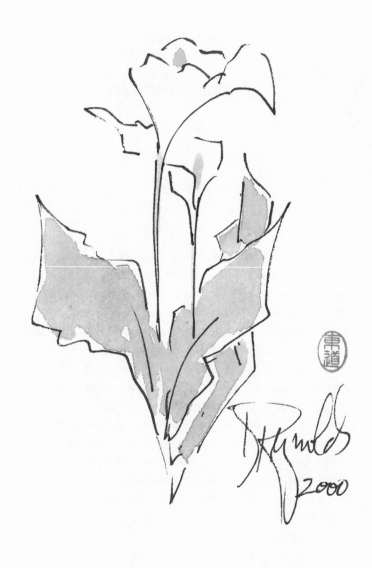

Dreaming isn't getting the practicing done or the studying accomplished or the résumé written or the clothes pressed. Narrowed thoughts of arriving home may cause a traffic accident on the way. Objectives are necessary, but not as substitutes for attention to this action now. Road signs can become detours. Please drive carefully.

The road and direction and destination are yours to choose. It's your vehicle, after all, sort of. Neither let others decide for you nor ignore their preferences altogether. The customs and values of those around you are road signs from Reality. But they do not reflect absolute laws. Criticism and praise and threats and ostracism are also road signs. Again, the vehicle is yours. Be prepared to pay the price if you break the law. Don't speed for the sake of speeding or park in no-parking zones just for a lark. Your vehicle must last long enough to get you where you are going. Take care of it.

32

꒰ ꒰ ꒰

Talking Yourself Seriously

*P*olitical and economic power must not be taken lightly or used in a self-serving manner. If your decisions affect the lives of the less powerful, don't isolate yourself from them. You can be in hell even while eating in fancy restaurants. Travel on an economy fare even if you can afford first class, especially if someone else is paying for your ticket. Refuse to be manipulated by fashion. I repeat, no one fools Reality. Hiding misdeeds from yourself and others is mere cosmetic covering of gaping wounds. What you hide from the law cannot be cured by medicine. Conscience bleeds internally.

Jobs end, businesses collapse, friends die, loved ones get sick, partners leave, bodies age, savings evaporate, children stray, dreams lurch, ventures fail, floods rise, security quivers, depression descends. What is there to do? Yes, what is there to do? Do it. Put your attention on what needs doing next. Do it. There is no other way to turn tragedy into post-tragedy. The passage of time takes off some of the edge, but it doesn't take off the responsibility for what gets done next. Wandering around in the mazes of why and shouldn't have and undeserving and could-have-been and blame and hopelessness and emptiness and complaint won't get the debris cleaned up or the crops planted or the car repaired. It isn't that feelings are unimportant; it is just that they'll take care of themselves. The myth of unfelt feelings is bankrupt. Failing to change the oil in one's car is no myth of tragedy.

Sitting and talking with a talking expert cures nothing. Relying on the expert testimony of a talking expert decides nothing. Grow up! Life doesn't come packaged in fifty-minute hours or fifty-minute court testimonies. It is easier to chat than to return to work. It is easier to hear a pseudo-medical summary than to look at changing Reality. It is pleasanter to hear that you need more self-esteem and more love and a better past than to hear that you are self-centered and unloving and lazy too much of the time. Telling the truth may not lead to popularity and financial success. Nevertheless, what needs to be done?

33

॰ॐ ॰ॐ ॰ॐ

Telling Tales

*B*ring me your neurosis and I'll fix it. Just hand it over. Bring me your misery and I'll alleviate it. Just pass it across the desk to me. You can't do it because what is yours is truly yours, only yours, is you. Where did your fear come from? What is the source of your obsession? Why are you so sensitive? Why do you worry so much? There are many stories told about such things. If you like the stories you may keep them in your mental library. But you needn't believe them. Stories are primarily for storytellers and their fans. You can outgrow such problematic mind-moments without stories. All you need to do is do your life well. Focusing on constructive living becomes your mind. That's good enough, you will discover. Why complicate something that is essentially simple and straightforward?

Stories take on a life of their own. She is lazy, he is unfaithful, I suffer more than others, she is neurotic, he is domineering, I deserve more recognition. The stories endlessly echo in space. We all have stories. They appear and disappear with changing circumstances and convenience. Keep them grounded in changing Reality as much as possible.

34

ॐ ॐ ॐ

Accepting Yourself

*Y*our past doesn't prevent you from living well. Neither does your race or your sex or your age or your diagnosis or your social background or your physical limitations. No one else holds you back. However successful you have become, something wants the best from you, expects the best from you, pleads for your best effort. You may ignore that voice; you may choose not to act on that voice; you may give up on yourself. The voice doesn't change its message. You can thank it or fight it. Your life is up to you.

Self-robbery and self-burglary and self-murder are crimes more common than you might think. Without walls of principle and habits of good character, it is difficult to keep the perpetrator out. Getting out of bed in the morning and making the bed offer an early start at building a strong fortress against self-invasion. Simple building blocks form solid habits of action and thought.

All right, Reality, I'm ready! I don't *have* doubts and worries and anger and sorrow and guilt; there are times when I *am* doubts and worries and anger and sorrow and guilt. I don't *have* sensory input; I *am* sensory input. This flow of conscious awareness isn't *mine;* it is *me.* What I am sent I become. The choice is resistance or incorporation. Why fight myself? When I'm hot, I'm hot; and when I'm cold, I'm cold.

35

ॐ ॐ ॐ

Self-Instruction

You and I share this Reality. Our perspectives may differ, but the Reality is one. That's why science works. Our minds were developed and informed by Reality. Our perspectives, too, are thanks to Reality. We share the marks of Reality's lessons about itself.

Obsession shields our gaze from the rest of Reality. To focus on anything implies ignoring something else. To notice is, in this sense, to be blind. So the difference between obsession and noticing lies in scope and purpose. Don't let your mind be velcroed to anything. Let something freely direct it from focus to focus. Shift your eyes and your balance with moving circumstances.

Repeating wise words as a mantra is no less an obsession than the compulsion of hand washing. Attention is misplaced in both cases. Let your mantra be Reality. Without drifting, without rigidity, flex your

attention. Snuggle into your situation and arrange it like your nighttime bedcovers. There is a time for learning truth and a time for trash pickup, a time to dream and a time to exercise the body, a time to eat and a time to eliminate. Devoting oneself solely to any single activity, however noble in itself, neglects the others. Be alert to what is presented to you.

You may not get the recognition and appreciation that your work merits. You may have to keep a low profile to get your best work done. However, no matter what others may think about you, you know what you have accomplished. You know what difficulties you surmounted, what ego and self-interest you overcame. Your very existence can be teaching. The finest praise is simply "You did what needed doing." The puzzle pieces that were you fitted Reality's puzzle again and again.

Lazy or thoughtless assistance promotes dependency. There is a difference between typing a child's letters for her and teaching a child to type her own letters. It is better to teach a child how to wash dishes than to wash dishes for him all the time. Modeling is different from exhorting. Neither hover nor abandon. Proper teaching requires studying your students and yourself. Proper teaching requires asking questions as well as offering answers. Do you see? Proper teaching ends when teaching is no longer needed. Proper teaching doesn't force students to remain students so that the teacher can retain teacher status. Proper teachers remember not only what they learned but also who taught them.

36

৯৭ ৯৭ ৯৭

Discovering Yourself

*T*here is a common misunderstanding that nothing can be done to improve our lives until we understand ourselves well. The misunderstanding holds that proper behavior emerges from insight and self-esteem and feelings of motivation. Such misunderstanding makes for meandering clients and wealthy psychotherapists. Insight and self-esteem follow behavior as often as they precede it. No one ever mapped the mystery from which behavior, understanding, evaluation, or insight emerges. Just pay attention to your circumstances and do what you know is right. Then pay attention to the results. Repeat indefinitely.

Those who make a show of piety and propriety seek to package a spiritual product. They seek to sell sophistry. Their goods are weightless. Empty boxes are empty no matter the gift-wrapping. You have the ability to evaluate the quality of merchandise. Shop wisely.

When people try to convey their suffering to you, how can you understand it? Even if you have the experience of your own suffering, their pain remains their pain alone. Their pain, translated into words and then translated again into your memories, never becomes your pain. Yet something within you responds to others' suffering. Why is that? What causes you to hurt when another hurts? What does it mean to go beyond yourself? Just keep on losing yourself in Reality. To do so is, paradoxically, the only way to find yourself.

37

ॐ ॐ ॐ

Making Strides

*T*he finicky and the slovenly share a common hollow core. They sometimes fail to greet Reality with open arms. If they can walk without falling down, they are capable of becoming intimate with Reality. To do so is neither easy nor hard. It just happens. All the while we call the effort "ours."

Take the time to make your own sturdy teaching shoes. After all, you will be wearing them daily. Plan their design carefully, then break them in leisurely, over a variety of surfaces. Find a balance between walking and resting. Otherwise, your feet may move, but you won't go anywhere. Reality will present you with students when you are ready to teach. Unready, you wouldn't recognize them as students anyway. Keep your shoes polished with reflection. Keep them flexible with action-based experience. Walk with attention.

Sometimes it is useful to step back and view the

larger panorama. But you can't walk across the street that way. The nearby cars are the ones that might hit you or give you a ride. They travel on concrete. No one floats across a street. Never forget how to walk. Wishes and dreams are a kind of floating. They have their place, but don't mistake them for walking. No one floats to accomplishment.

Some call themselves "neurotic." Some dream of being "cured." Some consider themselves "normal." No one thinks himself across a street. No one defines herself or intends herself or esteems herself or affirms herself to the other side. We all have to walk. Unescorted. Yet something walks us. Something attends to the traffic for us. Something moves us to cross the street. If you call that something "motivation," you have left your feet and begun to float. Step lively now.

38

꒰꒰ ꒰꒰ ꒰꒰

Getting to Know You

*W*hat is your history? What is your purpose?
Where did you come from? Where do you want
to go? Where were you before you were born? Where
will you be after you die? Looking this way and that,
don't forget to scrub your sink. Too long with unfo-
cused eyes makes for I-strain. Memorized maxims don't
get the bookshelves dusted or the carpet vacuumed.
Sometimes—sometimes, mind you—life is dusting
bookshelves.

To call thinking "the firing of brain synapses" is
either merely more synapses firing or more thinking. If
you choose to be in the loop, you remain in the loop.
If you choose to be outside the loop, you remain outside, too. "To choose" posits the same sort of tread-
mill. While attempting to figure out the sources of
thought, be sure to sweep the walkway and clean out
the garage. While wrestling with obsessions, avoid

wasting electricity. While experiencing anxiety, eat a proper diet. While engaged in these activities, thoughts will keep occurring. Thinking happens.

Shovels and forks and cars and gardens are all teachers. So are roadside trash and rabbits and printer cables. Some of their teachings are the same, some different. Study, study, study.

Science offers one way to study Reality's lessons. It is not the only way. Poets study, too. And painters. And meditators. Reality's mundane teachers have lessons individually designed for you. It is your task to discover the sinuous texts and commit them to experiential memory. You attend only one course. Until graduation.

Intertwine yourself with Reality. Wrap it around you until you merge with it. Permeate yourself. Become what is happening to you. Then go about completing yourself. In others words, do what needs doing. You can take credit for this doing, or you can pass credit along to others. What difference does it make? Reality's deeds get done. Nestle into Reality.

39

చిప్ చిప్ చిప్

Reality-Esteem

Some people would have you believe that self-pride is essential for a successful life. They try to brush onto their pupils a thin lacquer of transparent words. It is easy to see through such silliness. Self-confidence is earned through successful doing. Self-confidence, in the sense used by glossy people, is merely a small subset of Reality-confidence. Reality-confidence comes from noticing and purposeful action and attention to results, and then noticing and purposeful action and attention to results and so forth. More important than feeling good about yourself is doing what Reality requires of you. Layers of polished, shiny me-ness only blur your ability to see what each circumstance calls from you. You need not glow in the dark to walk straight ahead.

You discover who you are by doing what you do. You actualize your identity by action. You earn your own reputation. You know what you do. Where is the nobility in this approach? Where is the sensitivity? the spirituality? the keen insight? the empathic caring? You can't talk your way out of a paper bag no matter how much hot air you generate in the process. Flail your arms and rip the bag open. Clean your oven. Pay your bills.

Enter an unfamiliar room for a few minutes, then close your eyes and describe it. What you don't remember with eyes closed may be a blank, or the unremembered spaces may be filled in with imagined objects that simply aren't there when you view the room with eyes open. You remembered what wasn't there. Your mind made up a story about the room that made sense but wasn't true. Minds do that sometimes. Why do you suppose that happens? Do we exist by making guesses about what is—guesses that for the most part turn out to be useful, if not always correct?

40

჻ ჻ ჻

Vapors Condensing

We all talk too much, especially me. Talking coalesces mist into frozen cubes that look like Reality. Aimless chatter scatters such cubes about the room. Use your mist sparingly, purposefully. After all, it's not your mist. If you can't find the source of your mist, it's just because the mist is seeking the source. In any case, it's your mist. But wait! Are you misting contradictions in the mist?

The mind is the body is the whole of Reality. No one stands outside of it. You can't get outside of your pain or your dreams or your regrets. Swallow the bitter and the sweet of it while swallowing the swallowing. Then swallow the one who swallows the swallowing.

What can we do about obsessive thoughts? Just notice them and get acquainted with them. They are not merely companions, they are you. When they vanish they don't hide in the mist. They are completely gone. To think that something hidden within you makes obsessive thoughts is to create a phantom in the mist where there is only mist, misting mist.

As the birds fly through your windows, greet them with thanks. Even the dark birds who perch on your windowsill call out information from heaven. You need not feed or shoo them away. You need not aim for clear skies free of birds. Just become a bird watcher.

41

❧ ❧ ❧

Trekking

*W*andering means travel without a destination. Wandering moves you, but not to somewhere. Armchair traveling gets you somewhere without moving, but that place is merely the somewhere written about in books. Real travel involves destination and movement and happenings along the way.

Your journey leads through mountains and canyons. Keep walking. Exhausted or refreshed, keep walking. With eyes moving between path and scenery, keep walking. Alone or with others, keep walking. The journey is in the legs.

Your journey cannot be inherited or received as a gift. Yet your journey is also totally inherited and continuously received as a gift. Representing both recipient and traveler, carry your own baggage so that you can give it away. It wasn't really yours in the first place.

A train emerges from the tunnel without a sound.

Reynolds
1999

No engineer is apparent. No tracks appear, only tendencies and habits. Fast or slow, straight or meandering, the train disappears in the distance as another train emerges from the tunnel. What powers these trains? If you say "Here comes a train!" you do so while riding yet another train, looking out the window toward the tunnel. No one enters that tunnel. No one knows the designer of the train, the engineer, or the fireman. They were all born in the tunnel. No train ever goes in reverse back to its source. All trains disappear in the distance heading for other tunnels.

Also by David K. Reynolds

Books

Morita Psychotherapy. Berkeley: University of California Press, 1976 (English, Japanese, and Spanish editions).

The Quiet Therapies. Honolulu: University Press of Hawai'i, 1980.

The Heart of the Japanese People. Tokyo: Nichieisha, 1980.

Naikan Psychotherapy: Meditation for Self Development. Chicago: University of Chicago Press, 1983.

Constructive Living. Honolulu: University of Hawai'i Press, 1984.

Playing Ball on Running Water. New York: Morrow, 1984.

Even in Summer the Ice Doesn't Melt. New York: Morrow, 1986.

Water Bears No Scars. New York: Morrow, 1987.

Pools of Lodging for the Moon. New York: Morrow, 1989.

A Thousand Waves. New York: Morrow, 1990.
Thirsty, Swimming in the Lake. New York: Morrow, 1991.
Rainbow Rising from a Stream. New York: Morrow, 1992.
Reflections on the Tao te Ching. New York: Morrow, 1993.

Edited Works

Flowing Bridges, Quiet Waters. Albany: SUNY Press, 1989.
Plunging Through the Clouds. Albany: SUNY Press, 1992.

Chapters in Edited Works

"On Being Natural: Two Japanese Approaches to Healing." In A. A. Sheikh and K. S. Sheikh, eds., *Eastern and Western Approaches to Healing*. New York: Wiley, 1989.

"Japanese Models of Psychotherapy." In E. Norbeck and M. Lock, eds., *Health, Illness, and Medical Care in Japan*. Honolulu: University of Hawai'i Press, 1987.

"Morita Psychotherapy" and "Naikan Therapy." In R. Corsini, ed., *Handbook of Innovative Psychotherapies*. New York: Wiley, 1981.

Contact Information

For information about the nearest Constructive Living instruction and Constructive Living group programs, call:

New York City	(212) 831–6632, (718) 448–7142
New York State	(914) 339–9637
New England	(802) 453–4440
Jacksonville, Florida	(904) 389–3015
Cleveland, Ohio	(216) 321–0442
Kansas City	(913) 362–2119
San Francisco	(650) 712–0443
Los Angeles	(323) 223–1752
British Columbia, Canada	(250) 247–2032
Japan	(0473) 33–5830

To contact Dr. Reynolds directly, please write or call him at:

Constructive Living
P.O. Box 85
Coos Bay, Oregon 97420

Telephone: (541) 269–5591

Email: dkreynolds@juno.com, or dkr@post.click.or.jp

About the Author

Dr. David K. Reynolds is the founder of Constructive Living, an educational method for living realistically that is based primarily on two Japanese psychotherapies. He directs the Constructive Living Center in Coos Bay, Oregon, and lectures in Japan (in Japanese) for about six months each year on Japanese-Buddhist–based psychotherapies. Dr. Reynolds is the only Westerner to date to have been awarded the Kōra Prize and the Morita Prize by the Japanese Morita Therapy Association. He is afraid to fly and flies frequently to lectures and workshops. The watercolors in this book were painted by Dr. Reynolds while flying frightened across the Pacific Ocean.